FINE CHINA IS FOR SINGLE WOMEN TOO

FINE CHINA
IS FOR
single
women
TOO

LYDIA BROWNBACK

P&R
PUBLISHING
P.O. BOX 817 • PHILLIPSBURG • NEW JERSEY 08865-0817

Page design and typesetting by Robin Black, UDG DesignWorks, Sisters, Oregon, www.udgdesignworks.com.

Printed in the United States of America

Library of Congress Cataloging-in-Publication Data

Brownback, Lydia, 1963–
  Fine China is for single women too / Lydia Brownback.
    p.   cm.
  Includes bibliographical references.
  ISBN 0-87552-597-0
  1. Single women—Religious life. I. Title.
  BV4596.S5B76 2003
  248.8'432—dc21   2003048626

Dedicated to fathers, through whom
single women are made secure:

R. James Brownback Jr., beneficent giver of fine china
and exemplar of good taste
and
Richard D. Phillips and Philip G. Ryken—
shepherds of my soul
and
Almighty God—ultimate Father, Husband, and Friend

CONTENTS

ACKNOWLEDGMENTS

This book sprang from a seminar I conducted for some of the single women at Tenth Presbyterian Church in Philadelphia at the suggestion of my friend Meredith Riedel. For the privilege I have been given of sharing the joy of singleness on these pages, and for the hours she spent copyediting the manuscript, I am grateful to my mother, Wilma Lorraine Brownback. Thanks also to Barbara Lerch for her friendship and encouragement, and to the entire P&R Publishing team for their enthusiasm about this project. Finally, I am grateful for the love and faithfulness of Richard D. Phillips, Philip G. Ryken, Robert W. Kempf, and my dear friend Kelli Clifford, who were instrumental in restoring me to the truths on these pages.

INTRODUCTION

hy is it that only women on the brink of marriage get showered with household appliances, fine china, and Waterford crystal? Bridal showers were originally instituted to help a young woman get her kitchen outfitted with enough gadgets and cookware to prepare a decent dinner for her husband when he returned home from work in the evening. Today, bridal showers have become lavish affairs where guests select an expensive gift from the bride's registry at Pottery Barn or Macy's. (Today's bride registers at both stores.) But again, why is it that only brides-to-be obtain the desired goods for domesticity and dinner parties? Do married women cook more frequently than single women? Do they entertain more? In some cases, yes, but why should single women who do cook and entertain go without the items necessary for doing it well? They shouldn't!

In fact, such thinking applies to much more than dishware. That is because life doesn't begin when you get married. This is your life! You will never find contentment in living for what you hope tomorrow may hold. Contentment is for today.

CHAPTER ONE

LONGING FOR LOVE

*S*o you want to get married. That is understandable, because God created you to want that. The
desire for intimacy and companionship is part of being made in
God's image. After creating Adam, the first man, God declared
that Adam's solitary state was not good. He didn't merely say
that Adam would be better off with a companion; he specifically stated that being alone is not a good state in which to live
fruitfully. For many reasons, reasons we will delve into more
deeply in the chapters to follow, we crave the intimate bond
established between a man and woman in marriage.

First, marriage can alleviate loneliness, God's primary purpose for establishing it. However, there is a big difference between loneliness and being alone. Too often the distinction is blurred or merged. Discovering the distinction between the two goes a long way toward achieving the contentment God desires for you.

Another reason we feel the pressure to be married is that the culture in which we live tells us we must have a sexual relationship to be fulfilled, and for Christians, this can occur only in marriage. Therefore, we fall prey to the conviction of our culture, believing that without marriage we cannot be whole and complete—even in Christ. The church is not exempt from such cultural infection, and as a result, it has contributed to this misconception. We hear many a pastor pray for single Christians in the same breath as he prays for the sick and the dying. At other points down through the age of church history, thinking veered in the opposite direction. During those periods singleness was considered a superior calling. But today the infusion of the culture into the church has radically swung that belief to the other extreme. No wonder we are made to feel that something is wrong with singleness!

Another reason women yearn for marriage is that their friends are settling down, one by one, friend by friend. Either gradually or all of a sudden, panic hits, and a woman whose friends have recently married or plan to marry fears being left behind. The social structure changes. What was once a group of single friends becomes a group of couples, with the remaining one or two single friends feeling that they no longer fit in. The mutual confidences and shared experiences diminish, resulting in loss of companionship and social stability for those who remain single. That occurs because when a single woman is called out of singleness into the exclusive intimacy required in marriage, the close friendships she has shared with other single friends become necessarily secondary. It is often true that commonalities make for friendships, so when those commonalities are greatly diminished, the friendship fades away. When a woman experiences the marriage of several close friends over the course of a relatively short number of years, the perpetual search for new friends with common ground can grow wearisome and discouraging.

Women also want to marry to gratify a desire for procreation and motherhood. For that reason the desire for marriage can be especially intense. Like the desire for marriage, maternal yearnings are God-given, and because such longing is implanted into our nature, the inability to actualize it can be severely painful.

Finally, since God created us as sexual beings and pro-scribed marriage as the only legitimate means for realizing that aspect of our nature, our sexual desires increase our longing to get married. Acknowledging the sexual element in our desire for marriage is nothing to be ashamed of. In fact, God uses the desire for sex as a means of bringing a man and a woman together. Too often, however, when marriage isn't forthcoming, women (even Christian women) step outside the legitimate means God established for sexual expression. Always, without exception, heartache is the result.

THE LOVE OF GOD IN OUR LONGINGS

So if you are single yet longing for marriage, it is quite understandable! The issues we've looked at help us see why God's normal ordering for his people includes a non-solitary lifestyle. Yet since that is the case, since God's ordering most generally includes marriage, why are so many Christians single? Surely some are single by choice, but I dare say the majority of Christian women who are single did not choose that lifestyle. Some have never met a man they love or respect enough to marry. Some have never been pursued by a man they like and respect. Others have returned to a state of singleness through death or divorce. The important thing to do is get beneath all the speculation about why we are single and acknowledge the fact that each and every one of us is alone because, for today at least, God has ordained it.

Longing for what God has not given, or has not given yet, is not only reasonable and understandable; it can also be constructive as a means to draw us to cling more closely to the One who created us to hunger in this way. But living in a constant state of longing can become woe-is-me and self-centered. Most importantly, if we are constantly harping on what we want but do not have, we are declaring that God has not managed our affairs well, because with or without our longing, God wills us to be content in him. In fact, our contentment is of far greater importance to God than our marital status. Contrary to how we think, God also knows that such contentment does not hinge on whether or not we are married.

"Well, then," you may be asking, "since contentment does not depend on my marital status, how do I reconcile that truth to God's statement that it is not good for man to be alone?" (Gen. 2:18). When God stated that Adam's solitary condition was not good, he brought Eve to meet his need. But as we shall see, marriage is not the only legitimate and God-given fulfillment for our solitary condition. So if you are single, take heart. God has not forsaken you.

MAKING IT PERSONAL

Review

1. How do the following factors contribute to our longing for marriage?
   • Being made in God's image
   • Biological inclinations
   • Cultural influences

Questions for Personal Reflection and Group Discussion

1. Are you alone or lonely or both?

2. List or discuss specific ways that the culture and your Christian community have made you feel pressured to find a spouse.

3. Have your friendships remained consistent over the past several months or years? Or have life's changes radically altered your social structure? How have you responded to the changes spiritually and emotionally? What tangible steps have you taken to adjust to any changes?

4. Do you believe today that contentment hinges on your marital status? Be honest!

CHAPTER TWO

SAFE IN GOD'S SOVEREIGNTY

know a woman named Bridget who won't go to church on rainy days. That's because in extremely humid conditions her hair becomes an unattractive frizzy halo billowing around her head and face. Sounds ridiculous, doesn't it? But more than shallow vanity is at work here. Bridget is afraid that a hair out of place, or in her case several hairs, can thwart her hopes for a husband. Her fear extends from head to toe. Everything—wardrobe, fingernails and toenails, makeup—must be perfect at all times. Getting dressed each morning is intensely laborious for Bridget and takes at least two hours. What bondage!

Bridget is a slave to her appearance. It functions as a god over her life because she believes that a man will come her way only if she looks good. But as with all such gods that are not God, they never deliver what they promise.

Bridget's excessive concern for physical beauty has two underlying causes. One of those is our culture, which equates physical beauty with success, power, and happiness. In spite of possessing a different framework for life—God's Word—Christian women are not exempt from cultural influence. The other cause in Bridget's case is a lack of understanding about God's sovereignty. She sees her marital status as under her control. If she wears the right clothes, she will attract the right man. Conversely, if no one is asking her out, it must be due to some physical flaw.

CULTURAL CHAOS AND THE ILLUSION OF SELF-CONTROL

The truth is that no external feature or circumstance keeps a woman single or gets her married. The marital status of each of God's daughters is divinely decreed. And if God has called you to

<u>singleness, there is nothing you can do without stepping off</u> <u>the path of obedience to change that.</u>

Years ago I attended a church with a lot of single young people. We women spent much time evaluating the merits or lack thereof of the available men, and to my shame, I must say, we did the same about one another. Even in our thoughts we were sizing up the competition: "Is Mary more godly, more friendly, and above all—prettier—than I am?" Rather than giving us the stern rebuke we all deserved, God in his graciousness taught us all a wonderful lesson about his sovereignty in these matters. One day a new single man appeared on our church scene. Ben was intelligent, outgoing, and a born leader, and the single women took immediate notice. Whom would Ben choose? We all wondered and speculated. Surely he could have his pick. And soon enough he did. He homed in on Sara, a woman none of us would have considered. Sara was several years older than Ben, but that isn't what surprised us. What amazed us about his choice of Sara was the fact that she was overweight and unattractive in feature. But from the moment he met her, Ben had eyes for no one but Sara. And he really had to pursue her. She wasn't sure she wanted to settle down with Ben. But pursue her he did, and they were married six months later. My friends and I learned a powerful lesson: when it's God's timing for marriage, nothing or no one will stand in the way. Not our appearance, not the supposed competition, not our reticence.

But what governs God's ordering of our marital status? The same thing that governs all he does: goodness, love, mercy, grace, and his desire to conform us to Jesus Christ. Why would we want to change that? It is all for our blessing. In spite of that many of us do want to change it, and we try vigorously, whether it be through our appearance, our social activities, or even our choice of service among God's people. Yet sooner or later we discover that it doesn't work. In spite of our best efforts, we are not finding the relationship for which we hunger. Our efforts may widen opportunities for meeting more men; however, such prospects will come to nothing lasting, nor will they lead to real happiness unless God has ordained it.

BLESSED BOUNDARIES

The reason our devices fail is because God wants to show us that true contentment and joy in living are found exactly where he places us at any given time. God has ordained where we are to live and work out our daily lives. He orders whether we will be rich or poor. He has designed our physical assets or lack thereof, and the state of our health. And he has determined if and when we will be single or married. Around the life of each one of his daughters God has drawn the lines in which we are to live, and it is only within those lines that each of us can find true contentment.

The Old Testament book of Joshua contains several chapters dealing with divinely established boundary lines. In this historical account we learn how the Israelites came into possession of the long-awaited Promised Land. Once they were settled in the land of Canaan, through the drawing of lots God handed out portions of the land apportioned for each of the tribes of Israel. If you read Joshua 15–19, you will realize that God's big priority was not equal portions of land for each tribe. Rather, the lines drawn by God at that time were determined purely by his divine knowledge of his sovereignly ordered plans for each member of each tribe. Accordingly, a bigger portion of land would best serve God's purposes for some, and a smaller portion for others. Some were given established cities and villages while others were given uncultivated wilderness.

One tribe, the Levites, was not given any land; instead, its members were interspersed among the other tribes. But since the covetous nature of the Israelites, just like our own, demanded absolute equality as the price for peace, the Israelites made comparisons and complained when another tribe was given a greater or better portion than their allotment.

In an article that clearly articulates this portion of Scripture, a pastor named Dean Ulrich wrote the following:

> God will sovereignly direct your steps and put you in the place of service that he wants—however great or small. He'll take care of the opportunities for advancement, and He'll see to it that the things about which we worry so much will turn out well. For now, though, He's more interested in the fact that you faithfully follow Him in the place where He has you. In the future, He'll continue to draw and redraw the boundary lines the way that He wants, but He wants you to be faithful in the boundary lines that He has drawn now. We tend to eye up our neighbor's "property"—whether it be tangible possessions or skills, talents, achievements, friends, or looks. The next time you are tempted to eye

up your neighbor's property, think of these land surveys. They were "distributed by lot in Shiloh before the Lord at the doorway of the tent of meeting" (Josh. 19:51). Remember that God has drawn your boundary lines. Given your eternal hope—the fact that your hope in Christ transcends this life—you can say that your boundaries are pleasant.[1]

That is the key—looking beyond what we have or do not have today to see our lives in the light of eternity. The reason this is key is that everything about our lives has been ordained to lead to our eternal happiness—a happiness we begin to enjoy here and now—which is far greater than the fleeting happiness our desires provide. Once we have grasped this aspect of God's sovereignty, and as we are more and more conformed to his purposes for us rather than our own, we will be able to say, as the psalmist did,

> O, LORD, You are the portion of my inheritance and
>   my cup;
> You maintain my lot.
> The lines have fallen to me in pleasant places;
> Yes, I have a good inheritance. (Ps. 16:5–6)

The Westminster Shorter Catechism asks this question: "What is the chief end of man?" The answer given is this: "The chief end of man is to glorify God and to enjoy him forever." That means that everything that happens to us, every circumstance of our lives, is orchestrated by God to achieve those two ends. Therefore, if you are single it is because, for the time being at least, God has determined that you will most glorify him and come to enjoy him most fully as a single woman. If the time comes when those two ends will be achieved through marriage, God will change your life so that you will be married.

The same applies for women who are widowed or divorced. You began single, became married, and then returned to singleness again, all because God is working in you to glorify him and to enjoy him more thoroughly. That is not to say, if you are divorced, that God approved of the dissolution of your marriage. The prophet Malachi tells us that God hates divorce (Mal. 2:16). Nevertheless, he moved aside and allowed it, intending to bring much good from it in the long run. Author and radio speaker Elisabeth Elliot has been married three times and widowed twice. Her clear sense of calling in each instance comes through when she speaks of God's directing her life from singleness, to marriage, to widowhood, and back to marriage repeatedly throughout her adult life. Far from careworn and bitter, Elisabeth Elliot sees each change as God's particular calling for her at the particular time. Whether you are single, widowed, or divorced, God has already taken up the attendant loneliness, grief, or bitterness into his plans for your good and for the accomplishment of all he has planned for each phase of your life.

ORDERED IN ALL THINGS AND SECURE

So many women do not grasp just how sovereign God is. His control, his governing of everything that comes to pass, great and small, in the world at large and in our individual lives, is under his dominion. The Bible is woven throughout with the revelation of God's sovereignty. We read:

> Now see that I, even I, am He,
> And there is no God besides Me;
> I kill and I make alive;
> I wound and I heal;
> Nor is there any who can deliver
>   from My hand.
>   (Deut. 32:39)

The Book of Job shows us that not even Satan can touch us unless God first gives him permission. When Satan came to attack Job, he was able to do only what God permitted him to do. God set firm limits on Satan's activity in Job's life. Job experienced horrific hardship, and although he never learned the reason for his pain, he came out of the ordeal with a greater grasp of God's power and majesty. Before Job's painful ordeal was over, Job was able to say to the Lord, "I know that You can do everything, and that no purpose of Yours can be withheld from You" (Job 42:1).

Likewise King David offered this prayer to God:

Yours, O LORD, is the greatness,
The power and the glory,
The victory and the majesty;
For all that is in heaven and
in earth is Yours;
Yours is the kingdom,
O LORD,
And You are exalted as
head over all.
Both riches and honor come
from You,
And You reign over all.

In Your hand is power and might;
In your hand it is to make great
And to give strength to all.
(1 Chron. 29:11–12)

Psalm 139 tells us of God's intimate knowledge of us individually. The psalmist wrote, "Your eyes saw my substance, being yet unformed. And in Your book they all were written, the days fashioned for me, when as yet there were none of them" (Ps. 139:16).

Several proverbs recount the total control God has over people, places, and circumstances. We are told, "The preparations of the heart belong to man, but the answer of the tongue is from the LORD" (Prov. 16:1). And, "A man's heart plans his way, but the LORD directs his steps" (Prov. 16:9). Also, "The king's heart is in the hands of the LORD, like the rivers of water; He turns it wherever He wishes" (Prov. 21:1).

In the New Testament the apostle Paul said, "And He has made from one blood every nation of men to dwell on all the face of the earth, and has determined their preappointed times and the boundaries of their dwellings, so that they should seek the Lord, in the hope that they might grope for Him and find Him, though He is not far from each one of us; for in Him we live and move and have our being" (Acts 17:26–28a).

In Paul's letter to the Ephesians he wrote, "For we are His workmanship, created in Christ Jesus for good works, which God prepared beforehand that we should walk in them" (Eph. 2:10).

In these passages, and in many, many others, we learn that God is sovereign over the details. And the reason this is cause for rejoicing rather than fear is that his sovereignty is guided by his love for us. For those who have been reconciled to God through Jesus Christ, we can rest assured that in everything God's loving purposes for us are being accomplished.

FRIDAY NIGHT FREEDOM

That is why Bridget is free to shed her obsession with how she looks. If God wants her to get married, frizzy hair will be no barrier. In fact, very likely, God would bring along a man who considers frizzy hair beautiful. Bridget is free, therefore, to find more fulfilling uses for all the time she spends getting dressed in the morning. She needs to go and worship with other believers on rainy Sundays. She can make a run to the grocery store without makeup. When and if God wants Bridget to get married, he will bring the man into her life, and her appearance will have no influence on the outcome.

Like Bridget, many of us try to hunt for reasons why we are single, all because we do not have a proper grasp of God's sovereignty. "If only I hadn't made that stupid joke at the party last night!" "If only I'd signed up for that short-term missions trip! Linda told me that a lot of single men are going along." "Who will ever ask me out? I'm a widow with two kids and a lot of debt." We suffer needless anxiety because we believe that we can control our circumstances. We think that if we can manipulate all the factors in the equation, that if we try hard enough, we can fit our lives into the pattern of our desires. But when we do this, we are trying to play God. What we want and how we imagine our lives should be become our chief end, rather than glorifying God and enjoying him.

Eliza is another woman who struggles greatly with the anxiety that comes from an underlying attempt to control her marital status. She lives in constant fear of "missing God's best" if she isn't in the right place at the right time or if she doesn't want to date a man others are urging upon her.

Recently a man has been pursuing her, a man for whom she feels no romantic interest. And she is worried that if she cannot muster enough attraction toward him, if she cannot be more open, then she might be missing out on a chance to get married. Challenging ourselves along those lines is applicable for those who are tempted to get stuck on superficial issues. For example, some women insist that they can be attracted only to blond men over six feet tall within a certain income bracket. Going out on a few dates with godly men outside of those parameters, even if there is no initial attraction, is probably a good idea if they are hoping to meet a mate. A mind set on superficialities needs to be challenged and a more open mind developed.

But in Eliza's case the opposite is true. In her situation, such seeming open-mindedness is masking a subtle attempt to help God get her married. She believes that she is sinning if she cannot feel attracted toward someone. The crushing anxiety Eliza experiences daily would evaporate if she would embrace in her heart what she knows in her head—that God is sovereign over when and whom she marries. Like Bridget, Eliza is free to relax in the all-powerful, upholding hand of God, but her heart is afraid to relax its vigilance.

When we come to trust that God rules the details of our lives, that nothing we or others do can ultimately determine our course, we find ourselves experiencing the benefits of such trust. We realize we are free to stay home on a Friday night if we are tired, rather than fearing we'll miss out if we don't attend a party. We don't bite our fingernails or eat a pint of ice cream because we said or did or wore something that others didn't find especially appealing. We are free to be ourselves! Once we are unhindered, we can begin to discover who we are, the unique woman that God has made each of us to be. In many cases, our understanding of who we are is defined more by whom we want others to think we are than by the oft-hidden reality.

CRISES AND CROSSES

Yet even after we have reached a new place of trust in God's sovereignty and the freedom that accompanies it, even after we have come to believe that it is God—God alone—who determines our marital status at every point in our lives, we find in our singleness that the desire for marital intimacy is still as intense. Merely recognizing that God is sovereign is not the same as experiencing that sovereignty with the joy and contentment that he wishes for us. In order for that to happen we must also be willing to accept his ordering of our affairs.

I am saddened whenever I think of Abby, a Christian woman in her late twenties who is unable to experience contentment as a single woman. Abby has a well-paying job in the medical profession, and she devotes a good bit of spare time to underprivileged children. She enjoys swing dancing on weekends, and with her warm personality and pretty appearance, Abby is a sought-after friend. Yet her well-rounded life hasn't brought contentment. The warm smiles hide a deep and regular depression for which she has recently begun counseling. By her own admission, Abby is unhappy because she isn't married.

Some time ago I sat down with Abby and tried to help her see the truth of God's sovereignty over every aspect of her life. As our conversation progressed I was pleased to see that she already understood that God was in control of all things. So I asked her, "Abby, if you know that God is completely in control of your marital status, and that he will change that when and if he deems best to do so, why aren't you able to find peace in that?"

Her answer revealed the cause of her depression. She replied, "God might want me single for several more years or for the rest of my life, and I just can't accept that."

How sad. Lack of knowledge about God's ways is not Abby's problem. It is a refusal to submit her life to God if it means she might have to relinquish her ideas of happiness. It is rebellion, plain and simple. Her depression is caused by her rebellion, and she cannot and will not see that. Why does rebellion against God lead to depression? Here is why:

> Has the LORD as great delight in burnt offerings
> and sacrifices,
> As in obeying the voice of the LORD?
> Behold, to obey is better than sacrifice,
> And to heed than the fat of rams.
> For rebellion is as the sin of
> witchcraft
> And stubbornness is as iniqui-
> ty and idolatry.
> (1 Sam. 15:22–23a)

Have you ever thought about it that way? When we refuse to embrace God's ordering of our marital status or any of our other affairs, Scripture tells us that this is actually comparable to witchcraft—a practice aligned with Satan. In reality all active rebellion against God and his work in our lives has this satanic element within it. Is it any wonder, then, why our refusal to accept and embrace his lordship in everything ultimately leads to depression? Perhaps you do not realize that your discontent is just such a refusal. You may believe that you cannot help how you feel, that you have tried submitting to God, but it hasn't changed you. But your very depression is a reflection of what is going on in your heart. Elyse Fitzpatrick writes, "The truth about the choices we make is plain. We don't consistently choose the Lord because we don't really desire him . . . and we don't really desire him because we're not convinced that choosing him will result in our happiness."[2]

Some weeks after our first meeting Abby and I met again. I was astonished by the fact that she began our conversation with the same words with which she had begun the last one: "I've been depressed lately, and I don't know what is the matter with me. I want to get married, but nothing I try ever seems to work out. I just want God to bring me a husband!" Abby then went on to tell me all about her latest tactic—attempting to meet a mate over the Internet dating services.

Abby doesn't yet see that her refusal to accept God's sovereignty is the barrier to a full and joyful life. She reminds me of the rich young ruler whose story is told in Mark's Gospel:

> Now as [Jesus] was going out on the road, one came running, knelt before Him, and asked Him, "Good Teacher, what shall I do that I may inherit eternal life?" So Jesus said to him, "Why do you call Me good? No one is good but One, that is, God. You know the commandments: 'Do not commit adultery,' 'Do not murder,' 'Do not steal,' 'Do not bear false witness,' 'Do not defraud,' 'Honor your father and your mother.'" And he answered and said to Him, "Teacher, all these things I have kept from my youth." Then Jesus, looking at him, loved him, and said to him, "One thing you lack: Go your way, sell whatever you have and give to the poor, and you will have treasure in heaven; and come, take up your cross, and follow me." But he was sad at this word, and went away sorrowful, for he had great possessions. (Mark 10:17–22)

Abby's "great possession" is her own desire. And like the rich young ruler, she is walking away sorrowfully because she will not lay it down and take up her cross. If she were to do so, she'd find what Jesus promised the young man— treasure in heaven, treasure that begins here in this life the moment we leave our way to follow his.

From Coping to Contentment

So how can Abby, along with rest of us, trust God's sovereignty enough to lay down our desires and live as he has called us? It happens when knowledge of his control is blended with an equal understanding that his sovereignty is governed by his love for us—love that loves to bless and freely give us everything good. Jesus loved even the rich young ruler, in spite of his sinfully flawed understanding and refusal to follow.

Without a grasp of the depth of God's love, our understanding of his control may turn to stoic resignation rather than joyful peace. If we are not convinced that God determines our marital status in order to make us as happy as we can possibly be, in this lifetime and in the next, we will be left without hope.

All sorts of coping mechanisms kick in when we have a lopsided view of God's intentions toward us. One way we do this is by seeking to smother and kill our desire for marriage. We find ways to pour contempt on our longings so that we don't have to feel them too keenly. But in reality that is another way of trying to take control of our lives. We might pray, "Okay, God, if you want me single, fine. But please don't let me want marriage so badly. I'll be happily single if you'll just take the desire for marriage out of my heart!"

But God isn't asking you to crush your desire. He is merely asking you to cling to him in the midst of it. Nor is he likely to tell you whether you will be single for one more day or for a lifetime. Where, then, would be the impetus to hold fast to him? If life were certain, if we knew the future, we'd be less likely to cling to God for every little thing. That is why Jesus taught us, when we pray, to ask our Father to supply our needs one day at a time. "Give us this day our daily bread" (Matt. 6:11). That is why Jesus taught us not to waste time worrying about tomorrow, because, he said, "tomorrow will worry about its own things. Sufficient for the day is its own trouble" (Matt. 6:34). We do not know what God will do tomorrow. Today, turning to him for help in living with an unfulfilled longing is the work he has for you to do.

Nor does God want this to be a teeth-gritting ordeal. He wants us to live in hope and anticipation of what he'll do, today and tomorrow. And how can we do otherwise once we have come to know all these aspects of God's character? Not only is he absolutely in control over everything that happens to us, but also everything that he decrees for us is designed to reveal his love for us and his desire to bless our lives. The psalmist knew this when he wrote, "Delight yourself also in the LORD, and He shall give you the desires of your heart" (Ps. 37:4). If you trust in the true God you can know that, one way or another, he will utterly fulfill every desire you have.

MAKING IT PERSONAL

Review

1. Why did God draw specific boundary lines within the Promised Land around each of the Israelite tribes?

2. According to the Westminster Shorter Catechism, what is the purpose for which God gave us life?

3. Why has God predetermined the day-to-day details of our lives (read Acts 17:26–28a)?

4. Why are you single today?

5. What two responses are necessary on our part in order to experience joy in God's sovereign rule over our lives?

6. What attribute of God's character makes the fact of God's sovereignty joyful rather than something fearful?

Questions for Personal Reflection and Group Discussion

1. Are you trusting in something or someone other than God to bring about a change in your marital status?

2. How much time, attention, and money do you invest in your appearance? What is your motivation for doing so?

3. In what ministry activities or social events are you currently involved on a regular basis? What was your primary motivation for choosing these particular activities? Have your goals been realized?

4. As you ponder the truth of God's sovereignty over the details of your life, in what areas can you detect the presence of unnecessary anxiety? From what activities, patterns of thinking, and personal idols does your new grasp of his sovereignty free you?

5. What coping mechanisms have you adopted to deal with your unmet longing for marriage? What have been the results of adopting those strategies?

CHAPTER THREE

A RIGHT VIEW OF REALITY

A friend of mine, Tara, went through some difficult years during which she was involved with a man named Tom. He was a godly and kind man, and attractive too. In all respects, on paper, at least, he was a great catch. But not for my friend. Tara and Tom had too many points of departure to constitute a good marriage. He wanted to settle down in the suburbs and raise a large family. She loved an urban lifestyle and had little interest in raising children. His free time was devoted to athletic pursuits, whereas she preferred curling up in a chair to read a book. Such differences do not prevent a good marriage, and they were not the core of the problem for Tara and Tom. The issue was that Tara had trouble respecting Tom's thinking about most things, large and small. She disagreed with his interpretations of Scripture; she questioned his decision about the best travel route to New York City. Whatever opinion or piece of information Tom relayed to Tara, she found herself wanting to check its accuracy with someone (anyone!) else. As a result, Tara found herself resistant, and rightly so, to placing her life and future into the hands of a man whose thinking she mistrusted.

Tom wanted to move forward; the resistance was always on Tara's side. Yet they persevered, determined to make it work. They even tried counseling to see if that would enable them to establish a meeting of the minds. But the core problems remained unchanged. She wisely decided that the way to know God's will in her situation was to see if her relationship with Tom matched up to the biblical pattern for marriage. The apostle Paul's words to the Ephesians jumped out at her: "Wives, submit to your own husbands, as to the Lord. For the husband is head of the wife, as also Christ is head of the church; and He is the Savior of the body. Therefore, just as the church is subject to Christ, so let the wives be to their own husbands in everything" (Eph. 5:22–24).

Therein she found her answer. Was Tom the sort of man to whom she could submit her very life? If, while dating, Tara found herself constantly doubting Tom's opinions, convictions, and worldview, living under the authority of this man in marriage would be a constant challenge. Not only that, if she were to go forward with Tom, disobedience to God's mandate within marriage would have been all too likely. Tara, therefore, in spite of her desire to be married, desired even more to reflect Jesus Christ in every facet of her life. The Word of God was her final authority. So applying what she'd learned from God's Word, Tara ended the relationship.

Their friends were all glad when she finally did. The five-year relationship had been characterized by constant stress, breakups, reunions, and more breakups. So why did she wait so long before getting out of a relationship that was never peaceful or even enjoyable? Because she wanted so badly to get married! She kept feeling that if only Tom would change, or if only she could change herself, then they'd be able to be happy together. So she hung on to something that God wasn't giving.

Part of Tara's strong determination stemmed from the fact that during that time her younger brother got married. How hard it was to be the older one, the spinster sister! Even though Tara knew that she'd made a wise decision, the pain of letting go lingered long. I dare say it wasn't the loss of Tom that hurt nearly so much as the loss of hope implied by ending the relationship and the humiliation she felt. Would she ever meet someone else? How could she show up for family functions, especially when her brother and his new wife and their fabulous wedding were the endless topic of conversation?

Over the next several years envy infiltrated Tara's heart alongside her disappointment. While Tara remained single, her brother and his wife settled into a big house in the suburbs and became parents. Tara was suited to her more cosmopolitan lifestyle, but she envied what he had. Driving home from family visits she would think wistfully about how easy life was for them. They never had to worry about spending a Saturday night alone, or any night, for that matter. And how blessed was her sister-in-law to be a wife and mother living a life of domesticity—so much easier than the demands of earning a living!

Tara's urban life, formerly a source of pleasure, paled as she focused on her brother's big yard, so peaceful and quiet. So much room for gardening and backyard barbeques. Her little apartment lost a bit of its charm and appeal each time she made a visit to her brother's home.

Following such visits Tara would arrive back in the city where the lack of available parking spaces added to her dim view of the single life. Her brother had a driveway. She'd climb the stairs to her apartment, noticing city grime that was evident to her only after these family visits. And, she'd think, how nice for them to be able to throw their laundry in their own washer! No need to hoard quarters or harbor worries about getting an open machine at the laundromat. Over time the advantages of city living waned for Tara as she compared her single life with that of her brother and her other married friends.

It wasn't until she and her brother were spending a rare moment alone one evening that Tara's outlook changed.

Her brother was manning the grill, a task he anticipated as a means to unwind from the stress of work. Tara had gone up to visit that day and went out to keep her brother company while he grilled. As she felt the breeze and absorbed the suburban silence, she commented on how lucky he was to have all that. She admitted to him how she envied his life.

"That's funny," he said, flipping a burger. "I envy *your* life! Every waking hour I have is spent taking care of other people. I go to work and please my boss. I come home and tend to the needs of my family and this house. On weekends I have to grab all the time I can with the kids since I get so little time during the week. I have to mow the lawn and stock up at Home Depot. I have no time to myself except when I'm driving to and from work.

"You, on the other hand, have so much discretionary time! Once work is over, every weekend, every evening, is all your own. You can stay home, go out, cook what you want for dinner without considering what someone else wants to eat. You can sleep late on Saturday morning because there aren't kids climbing into your bed as the sun comes up. The grass is always greener, I guess . . ."

That conversation marked a turning point for Tara. She began to realize that she was so focused on the positive aspects of her brother's life that she had lost sight of the advantages God had given her. How often we see greener grass in another back yard! We look at someone else's life and see only the things we do not have. The "grass is greener" syndrome is merely a contemporary cliché for what the Bible calls coveting, or envy—something we will deal with more thoroughly in the next chapter. But how do we avoid the "greener grass" problem? We begin by cultivating a right view of reality.

Covetousness, or envy, is banished in part by recognizing that marriage is not the ideal lifestyle that we imagine. The process of moving from singleness to marriage is trading in one set of problems for another.

DEALING WITH DINNER

I recently asked a group of women to make a list of all the reasons they desire marriage. They listed several of those items we covered in chapter 1, those aspects of our nature that God has built into us. But in addition to those valid reasons—companionship, procreation, sex, intimacy—

the majority of the women mentioned things that reflect an idealized view of marriage. One woman, for example, believed that life would be easier for her if she had someone with whom to share the housework and other tasks of daily life such as paying the bills and getting the car repaired.

She was unable to see the reality, which is that housework and other domestic chores increase in marriage rather than lessen, even with an extra set of hands around to help. Oh, we might have a man to take the car for an oil change, but in marriage, breakfast, lunch, and dinner consume a great deal of time and energy, most usually for the wife. Meals are no longer a whim. Groceries, food preparation, and doing the dishes are a daily responsibility. And if there are children, all of that increases even more, as does the burden on a budget.

Contrarily, how do single women deal with dinner? If we're not in the mood to cook, we can grab take-out on the way home from work. (Along the way, we can pick out a video to watch in the evening without having to consider someone else's preference.) Or we can make a big pot of soup on Monday evening and eat it every night for a week. No one will complain about the lack of variety. As an aside, I must interject that I am not attempting to offer justification for personal selfishness. Unfortunately, selfishness is a temptation inherent in the single lifestyle. We single women must guard against getting set in our ways, eventually becoming callous toward or inflexible to the needs of others. Marriage is definitely a preventative to such selfishness, but if we are called to live outside of marriage, we do well to keep ourselves deeply involved with the lives of those whom God places all around us. While we are free to enjoy and appreciate the benefits that independence brings, God also intends for us to use our independence, time, and money in his service for the good of others.

Another woman's list stated that she wanted to be married so that she could have strong male leadership in making important decisions with finances, ministry activities, and handling difficult relationships. It is true that having an intimate companion is helpful in all of those matters. Such companionship is one of the blessings God intended marriage to bring. Yet the woman who wrote this on her list was unable to see the flip side of that blessing. Almost every one of my close married friends has told me that the most difficult aspect of being married is sitting back and allowing her husband to lead in situations where she believes her way of handling the matter at hand would be far superior. For women who are seeking to be godly wives, however, submission is vital.

Accordingly, the passage Tara applied to her relationship with Tom bears repeating here: "Wives, submit to your own husbands, as to the Lord. For the husband is head of the wife, as also Christ is head of the church; and He is the Savior of the body. Therefore, just as the church is subject to Christ, so let the wives be to their own husbands in everything" (Eph. 5:22–24). The apostle Peter addressed this principle of submission also: "Wives, likewise, be submissive to your own husbands, that even if some do not obey the word, they, without a word, may be won by the conduct of their wives, when they observe your chaste conduct accompanied by fear" (1 Peter 3:1–2).

Respect often means that when there are divergent objectives in matters large or small, except in matters involving a compromise of obedience to God, a wife must give way to her husband's leadership—even when she believes he is in the wrong. Many married women struggle with that on an ongoing basis, and it is one of the most difficult aspects of Christian marriage.

SAINTS, SOCIETY, AND THE SCRIPTURAL VIEW OF SEX

The desire for sexual intimacy ranked highly on most lists in the group, which is, of course, a valid and valuable reason to desire marriage. As we saw briefly in chapter 1, God designed us as sexual beings and gave us only one legitimate outlet for its fulfillment. Yet a realistic view of sex can help the single woman find contentment independently of physical intimacy. Society tells us we must have a sexual relationship to be fulfilled. Without one, we are told, we are unenlightened and one-dimensional women. Purity holds no value anymore.

Yet in the first few centuries of church history, the opposite was believed. Back then, Christians held abstinence in the same high regard that the enjoyment of sex is held today. Augustine, for example, was always suspicious that sexual pleasure, even in marriage, held one back from the deepest sort of relationship with God and believed that celibacy was superior to marriage. A few centuries later the reformers Martin Luther and John Calvin altered that view somewhat by stating that sex was all right so long as the primary motivation was procreation rather than pleasure. Not until the days of the Puritans did God's gift of sex come to be viewed positively in terms of pleasure and for the enhancement of companionship between a husband and wife.[1]

The bottom line is that singleness and marriage are high callings. Augustine and other believers down through Christian history went too far in negating God's good gift of sex, whereas today we esteem it too highly. Michael J. McClymond writes:

In North America, the multibillion dollar pornography industry unveils hundreds of new websites each day, young people engage in sex earlier and delay marriage longer than ever before, and countless households are destabilized or destroyed by infidelity. The secular world does not need to hear that sexual pleasure is good. Instead it is in dire need of people who indicate by their words and actions that bodily pleasure is less important than loving one's spouse, keeping one's promises, and seeking God's kingdom. And the unmarried can make an even greater statement against sexual idolatry than the married since perseveringly celibate people are a powerful witness against the culture's obsession with pleasure.[2]

God designed sex for marriage to more tightly bond one man to one woman. Because that is its purpose, we experience cursing rather than blessing when we indulge it—mentally or physically—outside of that context. Yet our sexual longings are much more than a mindset. They are a physiological reality, and in light of that, how do we cope during those times when the longings are especially powerful? We need to realize at a deep level that the existence of unfulfilled sexual desire doesn't indicate that we are missing out on something vital and necessary for contentment.

That is because God intends for sex to be fulfilling only within the context of marriage. Sex has no validity or worth as an end in itself. Sex is purely a physical expression of a spiritual reality. If we don't have a husband, therefore, we have no need of sex. When we are able to grasp this truth, we begin to understand that we are whole and complete in our singleness. We do not need a sexual relationship to complete us, to fulfill us, or to define who we are.

Unfulfilled sexual desire does not have to be a teeth-gritting ordeal. When carried to God in open, honest prayer, our longing can actually serve to deepen the intimacy in our relationship with him. This is why God often allows us to yearn for something over a long period of time: he wants to teach us to depend utterly on him alone rather than rely on the satisfaction that comes from his earthly gifts.

The Israelites experienced unfulfilled longing in the desert following the exodus from Egypt. Their difficulties in dealing with their longings caused Moses to write

> And you shall remember that the LORD your God led you all the way these forty years in the wilderness, to humble you and test you, to know what was in your heart, whether you would keep His commandments or not.
>
> So he humbled you, allowed you to hunger, and fed you with manna which you did not know nor did your fathers know, that He might make you know that man shall not live by bread alone; but man lives by every word that proceeds from the mouth of the LORD. (Deut. 8:2-3)

It is often as we experience the deepest hungers of life that we are surprised by God's provision.

TRADING PLACES

The reality is that marriage and singleness are merely two different lifestyles. God calls his women to both, which is evident throughout Scripture. One is not better than the other in day-to-day experience. Ask just about anyone who has lived for any length of time in both circumstances. Oh, each has its distinct advantages, but each also has its detriments. There are certain difficulties that you must contend with as a single woman that marriage will alleviate, but there are just as many troubles in marriage, troubles that you do not have to deal with while you are on your own.

So many single women see marriage as an escape from troubles, but don't think for a moment that married people don't wish for singleness at times. Single women long for blissful togetherness; married women long for a few minutes of solitary quiet. Single women see happy families playing together in the park; families playing in the park might not play at all behind closed doors. Single women often fantasize that marriage brings unconditional love and acceptance; married women find out soon enough that irritation with spousal shortcomings is an ongoing struggle. Single women look at marriage and envision hearthside snuggling in big suburban houses. Married women look at women on their own and see excitement, freedom, and the potential to realize personal goals.

There are particular blessings that belong to each lifestyle, but longing for happiness in a lifestyle that God has not called you to today leads only to an inflated estimation of the lifestyle you do not have. By contrast, appreciating the benefits of the lifestyle to which you've currently been called enables you to view marriage and singleness realistically. Remember that your single status can change any day as God decrees, but marriage is a commitment that by God's decree is to last for your lifetime.

MAKING IT PERSONAL

Review

1. How does a realistic view of marriage cultivate contentment?

2. How did Tara come to the conclusion that marriage to Tom was not God's choice for her?

3. While enjoying the benefits of a single lifestyle, what must we guard against?

4. What was God's primary purpose in designing sexual intimacy? Why, therefore, is sex pointless outside of marriage?

5. How does celibacy bring glory to God in our society today?

6. What is the result of longing for something that God has not given us?

Questions for Personal Reflection and Group Discussion

1. Have you, like Tara, clung to a relationship that failed to reflect the biblical pattern for marriage? Why did you linger in the relationship? What enabled you to leave? Have you had regrets about leaving? If so, what is the basis of your regret?

2. All broken relationships bring sorrow. If you have experienced such a loss, ponder the greatest source of your pain. Was it the loss of the person from your life? Or was it the loss of hope and potential to end your singleness?

3. Do you have a tendency to idealize a lifestyle different from the one in which God has placed you? Talk to a friend involved in the lifestyle you long to be living, asking questions about the realities of living it. Afterward write down or discuss those realities, making comparisons with your lifestyle today.

4. Make a list or discuss with a small group the reasons you would like to be married. As you do, write down or talk about the inherent realities—positive and negative—of each reason you mention.

CHAPTER FOUR

THE BLESSINGS
OF A THANKFUL HEART

roverbs 14:30 tells us that "a sound heart is life to the body, but envy is rottenness to the bones." What is a sound heart? It is one centered on God's ways in all things. A sound heart is one submissive to God's agenda. A sound heart is filled with health and wholeness. Contrarily, this verse lets us see that envy is destructive. That is because it is sin, and all sin leads to destruction. The result of envy is discontent. It destroys our delight in life. Envy is satanic because it is destructive to ourselves. It is also satanic because it is the opposite of submission to God; it is, instead, rebellion against his ways with us.

For those reasons we find God's prohibition against envy included in the Ten Commandments. The tenth commandment states, "You shall not covet your neighbor's house; you shall not covet your neighbor's wife, nor his male servant, nor his female servant, nor his ox, nor his donkey, nor anything that is your neighbor's" (Ex. 20:17).

SHRUBS IN THE DESERT

Covetousness, or envy, occurs when we set our hearts on something God has given to someone else. It occurs when our hearts resent that God has given to someone else something that he has not given to us. It is a determination to have that thing for ourselves, regardless of the cost to our neighbor. We are tempted to think that our envying is not coveting; after all, we reason, we do not want to take away someone else's husband; we just want God to give us one of our own!

Yet when our hearts are determined to have the thing we are set on, we do take from others. If we spend all our energy on pursuing marriage, we are taking away the energy that can be used to serve God, thereby taking something from him. If we latch on to an available man out of desperation, how do we know that God is giving us that man? How do we know that God does not intend that man for someone else? Not only does such sin rob God, but also when we covet something or someone, we steal from ourselves. We are robbing ourselves of the joy and contentment held out for us to embrace in the life God has given us today.

When we are discontent with our lot in life, with our single status, we are also inclined to jump at anything that might offer a way out. Genuine love for God and others is not what dictates our choices. Discontent clouds our vision and renders us incapable of making the best decisions. As we are discovering, discontent is the fruit of idolatry—an intense craving for something that we feel we cannot live without. The prophet Jeremiah understood how idolatry and its accompanying discontent keep us from the best:

Thus says the LORD:
"Cursed is the man who trusts in man

And makes flesh his strength,

Whose heart departs from the LORD.

For he shall be like a shrub in the desert,

And shall not see when good comes,

But shall inhabit the parched places in the wilderness,

In a salt land which is not inhabited." (Jer. 17:5–6)

If we believe we cannot be happy single, we will live barren lives and not be able to see when good comes. Such blindness will manifest itself in situations where a choice must be made about career, relocation, church attendance, and what men to date.

One woman I know of gave up a promising career, a set of supportive friends, and a good church to live in another state, closer to a man she hoped might show some interest in her if she placed herself under his nose. It didn't work, and after three years she returned home. What a waste of time! All because she refused to be content without a man and therefore could not perceive a wise course for her life. She chose to dwell in the parched places of the wilderness and therefore could not see the good in God's ordering of her life today.

The Oasis of Blessing

But it doesn't have to be that way! After his frightful description of those who look to man for happiness, Jeremiah goes on to describe the character of those whose satisfaction is found in God:

> "Blessed is the man who trusts in the LORD,
> And whose hope is the LORD.
> For he shall be like a tree planted by the waters,
> Which spreads out its roots by the river,
> And will not fear when heat comes;
> But its leaf will be green,
> And will not be anxious in the year of drought,
> Nor will cease from yielding fruit." (Jer. 17:7–8)

Notice that Jeremiah doesn't merely say that we are blessed when we hope in God; he says that blessed people are those whose hope *is* the Lord. Is God your hope, or is your hope centered only on the things you hope he will bring you?

When God alone is your hope, and when you are living solely for him, such faith brings its own rewards. We find these rewards in Jeremiah's words: an absence of fear and anxiety, the beauty of spiritual nourishment, and a fruitful life. Contentment also results, as Jeremiah pointed out, in the ability to experience good when it comes across our path. What he said was that when our hearts are set on having our own way, we are rendered incapable of seeing when good comes (Jer. 17:6). The good things to which he refers include spiritual and temporal blessings: delight in the fellowship of God's presence, the rich fulfillment found with like-minded and supportive friends, a Bible-teaching church in which to worship and find the love of family. These are a few of the riches that come to us when we rest in God's gracious ordering of each day of our lives.

Being content means that we are no longer held hostage by a hidden agenda within our hearts. When we are content to live as God has called us to live today, if we see that our boundary lines are falling in pleasant places, we are more discerning about how we spend our time and money, about our recreational activities, and about the men we choose to date. We no longer make choices based on the desire to escape our empty lives, because we have found that our lives are no longer empty.

CLEAR VISION AND SANCTIFIED COMMON SENSE

The apostle Paul wrote, "For this reason we also, since the day we heard it, do not cease to pray for you, and to ask that you may be filled with the knowledge of His will in all spiritual wisdom and understanding; that you may walk worthily of the Lord, fully pleasing Him, being fruitful in every good work and increasing in the knowledge of God; strengthened with all might, according to His glorious power, for all patience and longsuffering with joy; giving thanks to the Father who has qualified us to be partakers of the inheritance of the saints in the light" (Col. 1:9–12).

Paul prays here that the believers in Colosse would grow in spiritual wisdom and understanding in order that they might live their lives for the glory of God and be able to offer joyful thanks to God for the multitude of blessings he has bestowed upon them. Spiritual wisdom leads to tremendous blessing, but when we are discontent, when our hearts are focused only on what we want God to do for us, we are not able to discern spiritual things. That is because it is not God's will we are seeking;

we want our own way. By its nature, discontentment leaves us unable to grow in the knowledge of God's will because we do not want to know his will if it conflicts with our desires. If we are content, however, to rest in the boundary lines God has drawn around our lives, we find our hearts actively seeking to know his will and ways in everything.

God rewards those who seek him, and one of the rewards we receive is spiritual wisdom and understanding to discern between good, better, and best in all the choices with which we are confronted each day.

How many men have you dated for their great potential? "Oh, he isn't spiritually mature yet," you've told your friends, "but he's starting to go to church more now that we're dating." When we are content with our single status and trusting that God will bring along a mate if he wants us to be married, we find that such questioning and anxiety disappear. We are confident that God will make his leading clear, and we are content to sit back until he does. We will be looking for the best—God's best—which is always evidenced by the things, people, and situations that best pattern his Word.

I once read about a woman who was excited about a new man in her life. She talked incessantly about how wonderful he was but never seemed to give specific examples. So one day a girlfriend asked, "Tell me, what makes him so special?"

The infatuated woman answered, "Well, lots of things. He doesn't back out of our dates at the last minute, and he never makes unkind or sarcastic remarks about me."

"Well, actually," the girlfriend replied, "those things are givens. I asked you what makes him special."

How many of us have glamorized the basics because it holds out promise of escaping discontent and being alone? Even worse is the rationalizing of destructive relationships for the same reason. When we do this, we are like the shrub in Jeremiah, not the green tree thriving by the river. And we are not approving the things that are excellent, as Paul prayed, but instead are approving mediocrity or worse. Contentment with God is the key to spiritual discernment and knowledge, enabling us to hold out for the best, for our benefit and for the glory of God. Repenting of discontent, therefore, is an act of love toward God, and it also results in blessing for us.

FROM GRUMBLING TO GRATITUDE

But, we wonder, how can we repent of something we cannot seem to help? How can we avoid the feelings of envy that overwhelm us when our hearts yearn for something that someone else has? The good news is that repenting of envy can actually be quite simple. It consists in cultivating a thankful heart toward God for our lives as they have been ordered by him today, which requires submission to his ordering. Thankfulness breeds submission, and submission leads to thankfulness.

Sometimes—times when we do not feel thankful—the offering of thanks must begin as a pure act of will. Paul commanded this approach to thankfulness when he wrote to the Thessalonians: "Rejoice always, pray without ceasing, in everything give thanks; for this is the will of God in Christ Jesus for you" (1 Thess. 5:16–18). We see here that God wants us to rejoice at all times and to be thankful, no matter our circumstances. That means that it is possible to be happy single, even when we believe we cannot possibly be.

God commands our thankfulness because he is always working for the good of those who love him (Rom. 8:28–30). Even when everything looks and feels wrong to our eyes, God knows that everything is exactly how it is supposed to be. Perhaps you have heard the story about a little girl who went for a walk with her grandfather in the afternoons. Along the path of their daily stroll they would pass a shop featuring woven fabrics and tapestries. In the shop window was a loom that always held a tapestry in the making, and the two would pause to admire the beauty. One day as they stood peering into the window at the current work in progress, the little girl said to her grandfather, "Grandpa, I don't understand why anyone would buy that. It's just a messy pile of tangled yarn!"

Her grandfather looked down at her and realized that from her vantage point, she could not see what he could see. So he replied, "Natalie, you have a little person's view of this fine tapestry. You are able to see only the underside. But up here from where I am standing, I can see the other side, the side that will be displayed when the tapestry is completed, and it is being formed into a carefully designed pattern. The tangled yarns underneath are what enable the end result to look so beautiful." And he lifted the little girl up to his eye level so she could see what he saw.

Bound for Beauty

That is precisely what God is doing with us—weaving something beautiful out of the tangled yarn of our sins, our frailty, and our disappointments. We cannot see what he is making, but we can be sure the end result will make us beautiful. Our situation, therefore, is a necessary tangle underneath something beautiful. But it is not tangled from God's vantage point. Isn't that reason for thankfulness? We can rejoice and be thankful even before we see the finished work because we know that beauty will be the end result.

Even so, God's vision of beauty is different from ours, and it is his vision that is weaving the tapestry of our lives. The Bible tells us that true beauty is aligned with holiness. When God works to make us beautiful, his way of doing so is to bring forth true and lasting beauty from the inside out. This type of beauty—true beauty—springs from the fruits of the Holy Spirit that come to characterize us more and more as we grow in the Christian life.

The process by which we become beautiful in this way is called sanctification. To be sanctified means to be set apart from the world and increasingly set apart from our sin. But it is not just being set apart from something. Sanctification means that we are also set apart *for* something, namely, for Christ. As we become more thoroughly set apart we increasingly reflect his personhood, and the inevitable result is personal beauty, or holiness.

Holiness is God's overarching purpose for each one of us. It is his top priority in his dealings with his people. And since that is the case, our marital status is one of the means he uses to make us holy, or to sanctify us. We tend to view marriage as an end in itself. We are tempted to think that once we have achieved a certain peak of spiritual maturity, once we have overcome particular besetting sins, then God will give us a husband. But as we saw earlier, we cannot earn God's blessings, nor can we manipulate him, however spiritual the attempts may seem, to change our lives as we wish. But growth in holiness changes our view of all that, and as our view is transformed, genuine thankfulness wells up within our hearts.

The more we come to know God and to understand the overarching emphasis he places on personal holiness, and the more holy we become ourselves, the more we will desire what God desires for us. His priorities become ours. That is because in the process of sanctification, everything about us—including our priorities—is conformed to the image of Christ. Once that has happened, we can understand our singleness from that perspective. So long as holiness can best be brought forth in us through singleness, then God will keep us single. If marriage will better accomplish that in us, then he will see to it that we get married. So we see that marital status is a means to God's end with us—our sanctification.

That is why we can be confident that all things work for good to those who love God and are the called according to his purposes. Yet we needn't fear that such goodness means we must go without the good things that this life has to offer. Holiness and deprivation are not flip sides of the same coin. On the contrary, God's goodness, bound up with producing personal holiness in each of us, conduces to our happiness. God's goodness is as trustworthy and safe as his sovereignty.

Great Reasons for Gratitude

From beginning to end the Bible describes what God's goodness is like. In the Book of Exodus we read that God declared himself to be good when he passed before Moses: "The Lord descended in the cloud and stood with him there, and proclaimed the name of the Lord. And the Lord passed before him and proclaimed, 'The Lord, the Lord God, merciful and gracious, longsuffering, and abounding in goodness and truth'" (Ex. 34:5–6). Here we see that God's goodness is linked with his attributes of mercy, graciousness, patience, and truth.

The Psalms declare the power of God's goodness and how it always works for the joy and benefit of his people. In Psalm 31, for example, we observe King David pouring out his trouble to God and asking for his help. David appeals to God on the basis of what he has learned to be true about God, so he is able to say,

> Oh, how great is Your goodness,
> Which You have laid up for those who fear You,
> Which You have prepared for those who trust in You
> In the presence of the sons of men! (Ps. 31:19)

David knew from experience that God showers blessings out of the abundance of his goodness upon those who remain faithful to him in the face of great difficulty. God does that not only to show himself faithful to us, but also because others are watching. People observe how we handle our singleness, and those outside the faith will unwittingly assess from our conduct whether or not God is trustworthy. When God rewards our trust, however, it is not because we have earned it by our faithfulness. Rather, it is because in addition to the delight he takes in showering our faithfulness with good things, he also wants to show unbelievers that he does indeed take note of our lives and can intervene to bless.

We know from Scripture that it is God's goodness that leads us to the repentance he commands from us. The apostle Paul, in speaking to those who scorn God's goodness, wrote, "Do you despise the riches of His goodness, forbearance, and longsuffering, not knowing that the goodness of God leads you to repentance?" (Rom. 2:4).

Elsewhere Paul enumerated some of the blessings that spring from God's goodness:

> But God, who is rich in mercy, because of His great love with which He loved us, even when we were dead in trespasses, made us alive together with Christ (by grace you have been saved), and raised us up together, and made us sit together in the heavenly places in Christ Jesus, that in the ages to come He might show the exceeding riches of His grace in His kindness toward us in Christ Jesus. (Eph. 2:4–7)

Mercy, kindness, new life in Christ—all are God's goodness in action. And if it extends to the eternal securing of our salvation, then certainly the riches of his grace cover the lesser details of our lives.

The apostle James wrote, "Do not be deceived, my beloved brethren. Every good gift and every perfect gift is from above, and comes down from the Father of lights, with whom there is no variation or shadow of turning" (James 1:16–17). James makes clear here that God does not change. He always acts in goodness toward those he has redeemed. Do not ever be deceived into thinking that God is depriving you of something good. Your singleness, as long as it endures, is his good and perfect gift for you.

A grasp of God's goodness leads to thankfulness and it is also the remedy for hopelessness. God does not want to leave us hopeless, because hopelessness is a deathblow to contentment, joy, and a thankful heart. If singleness has left you feeling hopeless, meditate on what King David wrote in Psalm 27:

> I would have lost heart, unless I had believed
> That I would see the goodness of the LORD
> In the land of the living.

Wait on the LORD;

Be of good courage,

And He shall strengthen your heart;

Wait, I say, on the LORD! (Ps. 27:13–14)

David wasn't talking about a future, heavenly manifestation of God's goodness; he was confident that he would get to see God's goodness in his difficult situation in his lifetime.

Those passages are merely a sampling of all the Bible teaches us about the goodness of God, and each offers reassurance of why we can be thankful that we are single today. We can therefore trust that our singleness is God's active goodness toward us at the present time. And should our singleness ever become detrimental to our well-being, God will step in to change it.

As we begin to grasp God's priorities and his goodness, we will find the mere act of gratitude extending to encompass our feelings as well. As we begin to pray in all circumstances, with thanksgiving, as Paul admonished, before we know it, we'll *be* thankful for our singleness! God honors the act of giving thanks with feelings of thankfulness. You'll find that rather than bemoaning what you do not have, your heart is reaching toward God with real joy. That is the way that thankfulness leads to contentment.

Remember also that true gratitude begins with submission to God's will. You must be willing to accept the life he has called you to live right now. Such submission is an act of humility. Submission to God is, at first, a personal sacrifice because we are letting go of our insistence on having our way. But once we have let go, what began as sacrifice will soon be recognized as a privilege.

Begin by thanking God for the little things. When I began my personal exercise of thanksgiving, I gave thanks for the way sunlight illuminates the wood floors in my apartment early in the morning. I thanked him that my office has a window with a big tree right outside enabling me to see the seasons change above the concrete sameness of urban life.

We can also thank God for where we live, for our jobs, our friends, and our church. I would pray, "Thank you, God, that because I am single today I can say yes to the spontaneous weekend trip to the beach." And "Thank you, God, that because I am single today I have tremendous freedom with my time and money." Or "Thank you, God, that I live in a small apartment. I don't have to spend every weekend and each paycheck maintaining a large home." And, "I am privileged that you are using me in your service in ways that would not be possible if I had all the responsibilities of married life." After praying in this way for a short time, I felt truly thankful for all those things. Thanksgiving was no longer merely an act of will. The same will be true for you. I guarantee that when you commit to a course of prayerful gratitude, God will make you thankful for your life as it is today.

You will begin to see the abundance of blessings you have now as a single woman. In one way or another, God will open your eyes to see his goodness toward you in each aspect of being unmarried. You will find that you are no longer envious of your married friends, because you are able to appreciate what you have. You'll wake up in the morning eager to live out the life God has called you to live right now. And before you know it, you'll realize that contentment has rooted out bitter envy and a misguided sense of deprivation. You will feel exactly like the psalmist who wrote:

> Oh, that men would give thanks to the LORD for his
>   goodness,
> And for His wonderful works to the children of men!
> Let them sacrifice the sacrifices of thanksgiving,
> And declare His works with rejoicing.
>   (Ps. 107:21–22).

MAKING IT PERSONAL

Review

1. Why is envy satanic?

2. What thought patterns result in a covetous outlook?

3. How can we discern whether our desire for marriage is God-centered or covetous?

4. How does discontent exert destructive influence over our lives?

5. How does contentment sharpen spiritual discernment?

6. How does thankfulness result in contentment?

7. What is God's primary purpose in structuring our lives along set lines?

8. How are holiness and happiness synonymous?

Questions for Personal Reflection and
Group Discussion

1. Reflect on or discuss the characteristics of the tree and the shrub found in Jeremiah 17:5–8. Does your

desire for marriage make you resemble the tree or the shrub? Look closely at the descriptions of both to grasp how and why you come to resemble one or the other. Based on this passage, if your desire for marriage makes you more the shrub, how can you become like a flourishing tree?

2. According to 1 Thessalonians 5:16–18, offering thanks is God's will for us, no matter our circumstances. Do you offer thanks each day for your life as God has ordered it? Or are you grumbling rather than being grateful? Consider what lies at the root of your resistance.

3. Consider the most beautiful women you know personally. What makes them beautiful in your eyes?

CHAPTER FIVE

DAY BY DAY

*D*espite a substantial income and a strong domestic inclination, Carrie has lived in a sparsely furnished studio apartment for several years. She rarely entertains because there isn't anywhere for guests to sit. There are two straight-backed chairs pushed up to a small round table in the living area. But her decor has nothing to do with minimalist taste. With plenty of money at hand, Carrie has set out several times to buy a sofa but she never commits to a purchase. Instead she laughs off the empty space. "I'd rather have nothing than risk buying something I won't like once I get it in here," she says. But I don't think that is why

Carrie doesn't buy furniture. Carrie is desperate to get married. I believe she is afraid to make her apartment into a home because it will solidify her solitary existence. As long as she makes no investment in her home, she feels more poised to exit her current life and begin a married one.

A lot of women live that way, although subconsciously. Even when doing so would be a wise step, financially speaking, many single women will not purchase a home lest eligible men view them as too independent. Also in their thinking is the fear that after committing to such a major purchase, they might meet a man and thus be saddled with a cumbersome financial responsibility. So they wait and wait and wait, shelling out a good bit of income on rent.

Single women put a lot of things on hold because they are afraid that investing in or committing to or being associated with them might keep them locked in the single life. After attending five bridal showers over the course of a year, a single friend of mine had begun to envy the beautiful place settings, the Waterford goblets, and the flatware. She finally realized, "Who says marriage and good dishes must go together?" My friend entertains frequently and loves to cook. So she went shopping and selected a china pattern that she admired. She began collecting one plate at a time. Her family also enjoyed adding to her collection at Christmas and on her birthday. She now has place settings for eight, and the exercise of hospitality is much easier.

When the obstacle isn't financial, why don't more domestically minded single women do the same thing? It is because they are waiting for the bridal shower. Somehow they imagine that venturing forth solo into domesticity as maneuvering into sacred marital territory, a mindset that leaves them feeling left out of the good life. These women also hold back for fear that venturing out will more firmly entrench them in singleness.

LIFE IS NOT A SPECTATOR SPORT

But the truth is that we will begin to embrace life fully only when we realize that life doesn't begin when we meet our man—this *is* our life! It is passing by. Since God has ordained marriage as the normal course of life, the larger percentage of us will be married at some point in our lives, but what if you and I are among the smaller number who will not? Are we going to let the good life pass us by? Do we want to look back ten, twenty, or thirty years from now and realize that we have failed to serve God and have accomplished few of our goals, or worse yet, never set any goals because our only one was meeting the right man? I've known a few women like that, and they are bitter. They refused to see and lay hold of the happiness God was holding out in his design for them because they were set on only one way to happiness.

Jesus spoke a parable about frittering our lives away, wasting the precious gift of his earthly plans for us because we do not thankfully trust in his goodness. In this parable, found in Matthew 25:14–30, a man distributed his goods among his servants before traveling to a far country. He divided his wealth, called talents, in different ways. To one servant he gave five talents, to another he gave two, and to a third servant, the man gave just one. He gave to each according to the particular servant's unique abilities. Then the man left on his journey, leaving each servant to prosper that with which he'd been entrusted. Upon returning, the man called his servants to him to see what each had done with his talent or talents. Two of the servants had doubled what they had been given, and to each one the man said, "Well done, good and faithful servant; you were faithful over a few things, I will make you ruler over many things. Enter into the joy of your lord" (Matt. 25:21, 23).

But the servant who had been entrusted with only one talent, and by implication should have had an easier time investing it, did not receive words of praise from his master. This servant said, " 'Lord, I knew you to be a hard man, reaping where you have not sown, and gathering where you have not scattered seed. And I was afraid, and went and hid your talent in the ground. Look, there you have what is yours.'

"But his lord answered and said to him, 'You wicked and lazy servant, you knew that I reap where I have not sown, and gather where I have not scattered seed. So you ought to have deposited my money with the bankers, and at my coming I would have received back my own with interest. So take the talent from him, and give it to him who has ten talents.'

"For to everyone who has, more will be given, and he will have abundance; but from him who does not have, even what he has will be taken away" (Matt. 25:24–29).

In the same way we have been entrusted with talents, and we have a responsibility to possess them and make something beautiful from them. We need to view our singleness as one of the talents God has given us. We can invest it by maximizing the advantages to be found in it, or, like the unprofitable servant, we can bury it in the ground because we are afraid and because we believe God to be a "hard man" for giving us "only" singleness.

I referred earlier to the dividing of the Promised Land in the Book of Joshua. During this difficult process, at one point the commander Joshua found it necessary to admonish those Israelites who were afraid of embracing what God had apportioned to them. Joshua said, "How long will you neglect to go and possess the land which the LORD God of your fathers has given you?" (Josh. 18:3).

The choice is yours. And if you decide to start living fully as a single woman, not only will you find a life of contentment and joy, but you will also be honoring God. When we live fully within the boundary lines God has drawn today, we are exhibiting trust in his ability to know what's best for us. Additionally, others will see our joy and know that it is not because circumstances have worked out as we wanted.

We will be able to point back to God and say that he is our joy and our strength.

So start living! "Don't do something *about* your singleness; do something *with* it."[1] Are you domestically inclined? If so, make provision to exercise those inclinations now. Set a goal to outfit your kitchen, your dining room. Take a cooking class. Throw a dinner party, or have one or two friends over for a meal on a regular basis. If finances are prohibitive, there are many creative ways to do these things on a low budget.

Do you believe your gifts and talents could be put to better use with additional education? Then go back to school. Find a way to support yourself in the process and enter into a program of study. Some years ago I overheard a single young woman expressing to an elder in her church that she desired to pursue a doctoral degree. I was astonished at his reply. He said, "I wouldn't do that if I were you. If you want to get married some day, you are hurting your chances. No man wants a wife with that much education." This is precisely the thinking among some people, outside of and within the evangelical community, that can lead a woman to fear treading any path of prudent independence. But since God has allowed our culture to be shaped as it is today, it is an acknowledgment of his sovereign authority over the way things are to live to the fullest within its structure. The way God has structured our society includes many later-in-life marriages, smaller families, and more women of necessarily independent means. You can honor him accordingly by being your best, pursuing your opportunities, and being fruitful in the culture in which he has placed you. The elder who criticized the woman for her pursuit was seeing through the lens of a past era a time when God's structuring of society dictated a different lifestyle for women. He thus discouraged her from reaching toward the outermost borders God has drawn around her life. In today's culture, women's boundary lines are wider in many ways than in times past.

More important, however, than our personal pursuits is our service for God among his people. Ask God to show you how he wants to use you in his service in a way that would not be possible if you were married. Keep in mind that the particular areas of service he wants to show you are among the reasons why he has called you to be single! Do you have a heart for missions? If so, pray about what God might want to do through you to reach the lost. Don't reject opportunities to serve that appear to take you away from opportunities for marriage. Remember, God is in control of your marital status, so you have no need to manipulate your life to be in the right place at the right time. Make use of your unique gifts and talents where they best fit within the body of believers in which God has placed you, even if it appears that doing so will limit your options to meet a man. God will show you just how powerful he is as you live in faith in his sovereignty and goodness.

GOD'S WAY TO THE GOOD LIFE

In my early thirties I was part of a large group of single Christians. We spent all of our free time together, participating in church activities and enjoying weekend recreation. Yet, one by one, my closest friends within that group paired off and got married. Those of us who were left continued to do the things the larger group had always done, yet it became rote, a mere going through the motions. What was the purpose of it all, I wondered. What were we accomplishing? It seemed as if we were merely filling up the empty places in our lives as best we could. We all thought that if we followed our friends into marriage, our lives would take on purpose once again. It was at that point that I hit rock-bottom discontent with my single status, because I mistakenly thought that marriage would restore meaning to my life. After all, so many of my friends were advancing into this next phase of life and were occupied with home buying and having children. Their path seemed the natural course of life. I thought that somehow I'd fallen off the track.

It was at that point, weary with the weekend sameness, that I prayed in earnest about what God might want to do with my life and my time. "Lord," I prayed, "if not marriage right now, then what?" God had allowed me to sink to a point where I was open to his way, and it was during the next week that the inclination to write about God and his Word took hold. I stopped the social routine and began writing. Over the next two years, God opened doors through my writing; then suddenly one day I realized that my former sense of futility was gone. I was completely fulfilled; God had cultivated in me a tremendous sense of purpose. I no longer see marriage as the only road to the good life. I am completely fulfilled by all God has given me, and I see that his will is good, acceptable, and perfect in ways that I wasn't open to seeing before.

I think that, as women, we often mistakenly equate marriage with purpose and usefulness. However when we discover and live out the plans God has for us, that link comes into correct focus. All that it takes is a willingness to live our lives God's way. When you reach that point, you too will find that nothing is missing. So if you find yourself questioning your purpose, if day-to-day life seems futile, take your questions to God.

Ask God to provide his remedy for you. He will bring people into your life who are also in need of companionship. Usually the best means of overcoming loneliness is to get out and meet someone else's need. There are lonely people everywhere! It could be that you are in a position to provide a home for someone, even on a temporary basis.

Are you longing for children? Then get involved in children's ministry activities or offer to babysit for your pastors' children. A single woman I know took that a step further by deciding to investigate foster parenting. She has completed the necessary training and is now in a position to provide a loving, if temporary, home to a needy, neglected child.

Far from keeping marriage out of reach, such actions could be the vehicle God uses to widen your boundary lines, even into marriage. We only need to remember that if he wants us to be married, it will happen. If marriage is not what he has for you, that is because he has something better suited for you. Whatever that may entail is not a second-best plan; God knows it will make you happier than marriage would. We need not fear that tying ourselves down in acts of service—loving others and providing for their needs—will necessarily take us off the marriage market. On the contrary, when we are living life to the fullest, using all God has given us today, that is often when God opens other doors as well.

Review

1. How can embracing our singleness bring glory to God, generally and specifically?

2. What can hinder us from experiencing the joys of a single life?

3. How can serving God to the fullest result in blessing for ourselves and others?

Questions for Personal Reflection and Group Discussion

1. Do you refrain from particular activities, purchases, or pursuits because you are afraid that going ahead with them will entrench you in a life of singleness? Do you view certain pursuits as valid only in the realm of sacred marital territory? What concrete steps can you take in your life to break out of this mindset?

2. How are you presently using your gifts and talents to serve God and the people he has placed in your life?

How have you decided where and how to apply yourself? How much has prayerful consideration and wise counsel contributed to your decisions? What other considerations influence your use of your talents?

CHAPTER SIX

UNDERSTANDING
YOUR UNIQUE ADVANTAGES

*B*elieve it or not, being set apart for singleness is a privilege. Not everyone has such a unique opportunity for more than a brief span of life. We train our minds to believe that we are single due to some inherent inadequacy when in reality it is because God wants us all to himself for a season, be it one more week, another year, or a lifetime. Singleness is a special blessing, a privileged calling.

You will never have more time to devote to studying God's Word and praying than you do while you are single. Nor will you otherwise have the same freedom to serve God exclusively. Doesn't it thrill your heart that he is keeping you set apart just for him? In a letter the apostle Paul wrote to the believers at the church in Corinth, he focused specifically on single women. He wrote, "There is a difference between a wife and a virgin. The unmarried woman cares about the things of the Lord, that she may be holy both in body and in spirit. But she who is married cares about the things of the world—how she may please her husband" (1 Cor. 7:34). Paul went on to explain that he was not seeking to rob the Corinthians of the good things life has to offer. Rather, "this I say for your own profit, not that I may put a leash on you, but for what is proper, and that you may serve the Lord without distraction" (1 Cor. 7:35). Dr. Philip Graham Ryken said,

Jeremiah is an example of what Paul was talking about in 1 Corinthians 7. The Lord wanted Jeremiah's undivided attention. He wanted his prophet to be concerned about nothing else except pleasing God, and especially so because he lived in a time of spiritual crisis. We need more of that kind of godly singleness in the church. The Bible teaches that singleness is an opportunity to be more devoted to Christ and less devoted to the world. Too many Christian singles have just the opposite attitude. Too many are overmuch concerned about the affairs of this world, and not concerned enough about the affairs of Christ.

If you are single, do not be single for the lack of something better to do. Be single to the glory of God, undivided in your devotion to him. You have the freedom and the time, often the money, to take bold adventures in the name of Jesus Christ. You can do things that would be unwise or impossible for married Christians to do. And if the days are evil, then godly singles should be the strength of the church. Singleness is not a curse; it is a blessing both to the single individual and to the church. A Christian is not single by default as if he or she is waiting for something or someone better to come along. A Christian is called to be single to the glory of God as long as he or she is single—either until marriage or death, whichever comes first. Singleness is not an accident. It is not a misfortune. It is a divine calling.[1]

FATHER, FRIEND, AND HUSBAND

According to Paul, as single women we are in a unique position to offer our whole selves, body and spirit, to God. The result is a companionship with God from which married women are distracted. It is not that married women are shut out from such fellowship with God, but rather that we single women have more opportunity to experience him directly as father, friend, and husband. God will provide from himself and from within the church what we lack in male headship and protection over our lives in ways great and small.

I confess that I have an unholy fear of insects. I live in dread of crossing paths with the large cockroaches so prevalent in the city where I live. When I moved into my apartment, I expressed my fear to God, asking him to act as the man of the house and keep all such creatures out of my home. Rather than rebuking me for being afraid, God answered my prayer in a most creative and gentle way. On two separate occasions, one of these big roaches appeared, crawling on my wall. Both times the roach was of the two-inch-long variety that has the capability to fly short distances. When approached by humans these roaches make clacking noises, quite frightening for bug phobics, I assure you. But on both occasions I had a male visitor sitting in the living room with me, and in each case my guest did the chivalrous thing by removing it. God not only protected me from the necessity of removing the roach single-handedly; he even guarded me from the fear I would have felt if I'd come across it by myself. Both times it was my visiting friend who spotted the bug before I did and gently informed me of its presence in the room. Through that lesson I learned how in big matters and small God will shield you and provide all you need.

FREEDOM OR FETTERS IN THE AFFAIRS OF THIS LIFE

Being set apart for God also enables us to serve God unhindered in a greater diversity of ways than married women can. A wife and mother's primary means of serving is the care and nurture of her husband and children, and when this is done thoroughly and well, there is little time left for other types of service. As a single woman I have time to write books, lead one or two women's Bible studies, make meals for families in my church, and work full time. Paul was clear: marriage forces women to focus on the affairs of this life. To do otherwise in marriage means that we are not fulfilling our marriage vows. Focusing elsewhere—even on ministry activities—can interfere with the married woman's primary calling as wife and mother. It is an act of obedience for a married woman to serve God and her family; obedience for the single woman lies solely in serving God.

In this same discourse Paul also said of marriage,

> Now concerning virgins: I have no commandment from the Lord; yet I give judgment as one whom the Lord in His mercy has made trustworthy. I suppose therefore that this is good because of the present distress [literally, "the present necessity"]—that it is good for a man to remain as he is: Are you bound to a wife? Do not seek to be loosed. Are you loosed from a wife? Do not seek a wife. But even if you do marry, you have not sinned; and if a virgin marries, she has not sinned.

Nevertheless such will have trouble in the flesh, but I would spare you. (1 Cor. 7:25–28)

"Trouble in the flesh." What did Paul mean? He was talking about the realities of marriage that we looked at in chapter 4: the difficulties that come from living so intimately with another fallen human being, and the requirement to forego personal goals, however lofty, for the sake of another. Paul, single at least for the portion of his life to which we are exposed in Scripture, had a realistic view of marriage and singleness, and in 1 Corinthians he points out the advantages of remaining unmarried. Singleness is not necessarily preferable to marriage. Each calling serves its purpose, and we must give careful thought to how we are best suited to serve God. It could be that when Paul referred to "the present distress," he was advising against marriage because of a specific problem facing the Corinthian church. Yet in looking at the passage as a whole, it is just as likely that he was referring more generally to the predicament that all Christians face as they seek to live for Christ. About this passage Susan Foh writes,

Though Paul considers motherhood important and appropriate for Christian women, he did not believe a husband and family were necessary to fulfill everyone. In the Old Testament, marriage seemed to be the accepted lot of everyone and not much is said about singleness. Paul, on the other hand, legitimizes, even exalts, the position of single men and women (1 Cor. 7:25–38). In this respect, he is more progressive in his thinking than modern society, which still looks with pity and/or disdain on spinsters. Paul says that the unmarried can better serve Christ, and so he recommends staying single. The married have divided concerns, to please Christ and to please their spouses, so that singleness is an asset for service to the Lord.[2]

NO MORE FEARS

Are you afraid to look too closely at Paul's advice? Maybe you are scared of considering his teaching because to do so means facing the possibility that a lifetime of singleness is a good and acceptable calling—perhaps for you. Many women I know cling exclusively to God's words in Genesis 2:18, "It is not good that man should be alone." Because of God's assessment there, these women are sure that God intends to bring them into marriage. But anchoring in the harbor of this verse alone is to rest on false hope. We cannot isolate one portion of Scripture to suit our desires and banish our fears, however tempting that may be. The only way to find contentment in God's ways is to seek to understand all of his teaching on a given subject and then to accept all we find as the complete truth. In the case of marriage, we see from the whole of Scripture that marriage and singleness are good and godly. Again, it all comes down to what God has determined is best suited for what he wants to do with and for you.

Reread Paul's words with an eye to your distinct advantages as a single woman. What does he say? You are freed from a measure of care—yes, difficulty—that married woman are called to undertake. We find many examples in the New Testament. Mary Magdalene was single, and this freed her to follow Jesus wherever he went, listening to his teaching, tending to his earthly needs, and learning to love him. She was there at the cross when her beloved Lord was crucified. It was Mary to whom Jesus first appeared on the morning of his resurrection (Mark 16:9).

Anna, a woman widowed after only seven years of marriage, subsequently devoted all her time to companionship with God through prayer and fasting in the temple. As a result, she was there the day Mary and Joseph brought the infant Jesus into the temple to present him to the Lord. Anna saw firsthand the fulfillment of all her prayers (see Luke 2:22–38).

Lydia, most likely a single woman, was free to open her home to the apostles. If she'd had a husband to consider, such hospitality may not have been possible. As it was, she refreshed the weary apostles with warm hospitality, and as a result she received direct exposure to the teaching about God's kingdom and living the life of faith (see Acts 16:11–15, 40).

Each of these women had opportunities to know the Lord and advantages to serve him that would have been hindered had they been married. The same is true for you. If you are single, it is because, like Mary, Anna, and Lydia, God has unique opportunities and advantages to give to you, as well, advantages that wouldn't be possible apart from your single status. That is cause for gratitude and rejoicing! Ask God to fulfill his purposes in your singleness, and he surely will.

MAKING IT PERSONAL

Review

1. Why is singleness a privilege?

2. In what ways is a single woman less encumbered than a married woman?

3. What can we infer from considering Genesis 2:18 and 1 Corinthians 7:34–35?

Questions for Personal Reflection or Group Discussion

1. Is your desire for marriage subordinate to your desire to serve God? In other words, can you honestly and openly pray through Paul's advice in 1 Corinthians 7, asking God to shape your life in its entirety so as to best glorify and enjoy him?

CHAPTER SEVEN

ESTABLISHING
A CHRIST-CENTERED LIFE

odliness with contentment is great gain," wrote the apostle Paul to Timothy. "For we brought nothing into this world, and it is certain that we can carry nothing out. And having food and clothing, with these we shall be content. But those who desire to be rich [craving the things of this world] fall into temptation and a snare, and into many foolish and harmful lusts which drown men in destruction and perdition" (1 Tim. 6:6–9).

We can see clearly from Paul's words to Timothy that contentment carries with it its own reward. If our hearts are set on the things of God, the things of this life don't seem so crucial to our happiness. As Paul wisely points out, anything we obtain here and now will only have to be given up in the long run. Why labor for what won't last? Since Paul's entire life was given over to the things of God, he was able to look at his meager earthly possessions and find contentment in the fact that he had even those things. Food and clothing were enough for him because his heart was set on the greatest treasure of all.

Very likely you have much more than food and clothing. In addition to food and clothing you likely have friends, a job (or the skills to find one), an education, a home, and a family of one sort or another—either a biological one or one provided for you by God among other believers. When you are truly content, your craving for more will dissipate. If your heart has been set on God, the resulting contentment enables you to see all these extras as icing on the cake of your life.

Looking in All the Right Places

Paul did not achieve contentment of this depth by snuffing out his personal desires. On the contrary, he pursued what he wanted wholeheartedly and received what he was after. That's because the thing Paul wanted most was Jesus Christ and his glory. From his words of encouragement to Timothy, it is evident that earthly things had come to mean little to Paul in comparison with Christ and having a relationship with God. That is why the barest necessities were sufficient for him.

Yet we still ask, how could Paul speak of contentment in the face of so much suffering? He had experienced deprivation, hardship, persecution, and poverty. Nevertheless, he was a contented man. Contentment was something God cultivated in Paul through the trials he faced; that is the same way God cultivates it in us. It is an asset to be learned, in Paul's case and in ours. He wrote, "I have learned in whatever state I am, to be content: I know how to be abased, and I know how to abound. Everywhere and in all things I have learned both to be full and to suffer need. I can do all things through Christ who strengthens me" (Phil. 4:11–13).

As we can see, contentment is a learned thing. Often it comes only through difficulties of one sort or another. For Paul it came through the loss of personal power, criticism and ridicule from false teachers, deprivation of life's basic necessities, and an unhealed thorn in his flesh

(2 Cor. 10:10–12). As for you and me, we might learn contentment through the experience of watching our friends get married one by one, through an awareness that our chances for motherhood diminish as the years sweep by, or through the pain of loneliness.

When Paul was plagued by the thorn in his flesh, he asked the Lord on three separate occasions to remove the thorn. What did Jesus answer? He said, "My grace is sufficient for you, for My strength is made perfect in weakness" (2 Cor. 12:9). And through this grace, Paul learned to be content in the knowledge that he could do all things through Christ who strengthened him (Phil. 4:13). God had a reason for not removing Paul's thorn: it was to keep Paul humble enough to be an effective ambassador for Christ. Very likely, in a manner similar to Paul's, you have asked God to remove the thorn of singleness. And if God has said no, it is only that you might learn that his grace is sufficient for you and to keep you able to serve him in the way he alone knows is best.

Paul not only learned that the grace of God is sufficient for his every trial and trouble and that Christ was his strength in all circumstances. He also experienced that grace and strength from a position of great joy. It is one thing to believe something is true; it is another to embrace it to the extent that it causes us to overflow with joy. But Paul did just that: his goal, his chief end, his reason for living had come to be nothing else but Jesus Christ.

Christ was the source of Paul's strength, and in addition his whole life was oriented around pleasing God. Whether he lived with or without particular earthly blessings, Paul was content because Christ was his life. And so we see that contentment is not something elusive, just beyond our grasp. Contentment goes hand in hand with the Christ-centered life. It is readily available to us now. It is merely a matter of reorienting our lives around Jesus.

THE SPIRITUAL LAW OF INCREASING RETURNS

When we do orient our lives around Jesus, our outlook will be similar to Paul's. From the moment of his conversion on the road to Damascus, he no longer lived for his own hopes, dreams, and goals. All that he had previously based his life upon was cast behind him, which was no small loss by earthly standards. Look at the characteristics of Paul's life before his conversion: "If anyone else thinks he may have confidence in the flesh, I more so: circumcised the eighth day, of the stock of Israel, of the tribe of Benjamin, a Hebrew of the Hebrews; concerning the law, a Pharisee; concerning zeal, persecuting the church; concerning the righteousness which is in the law, blameless" (Phil. 3:4–6). Very impressive credentials by the worldly standards of his day. When he committed himself to Christ, he was able to let all that go, because Christ became his only goal.

Paul went on, in his letter to the Philippians, to say that what he had gained was far greater than anything he had left behind. He wrote, "But what things were gain to me, these I have counted loss for Christ. Yet indeed I also count all things loss for the excellence of the knowledge of Christ Jesus my Lord, for whom I have suffered the loss of all things, and count them as rubbish, that I may gain Christ and be found in him" (Phil. 3:7–9a).

Paul was trying to impress upon his readers that nothing compares with the joy of making Christ the center of one's life. God desires that you come to the same place. He wants you to be able to say, "What things were gain to me—my attractive appearance, my education, my career, a large singles fellowship in which to meet a mate, my dream of marriage, a home in the suburbs—I count them as rubbish, that I may gain Christ and be found in him."

Does that sound impossible to you? It won't be impossible if you are looking at God, if you seek to make him the center of your affections. If you actively pursue a Christ-centered focus in all you are and do, you will find your mind and heart being transformed to desire him above anything else. Do not be discouraged if a mindset like Paul's seems out of reach for you. Even Paul knew he had a long way to go, in spite of how far God had already brought him. That is why he immediately went on to write, "Brethren, I do not count myself to have apprehended; but one thing I do, forgetting those things which are behind and reaching forward to those things which are ahead, I press toward the goal for the prize of the upward call of God in Christ Jesus" (Phil. 3:13–14).

Perhaps the best way for you to begin reaching forward is to ask God to help you even to desire a Christ-centered heart. So much of the time we want Christ, but we want him along with so many other things besides. Ask God to make Christ the deepest longing, the one thing above all else that you yearn for. Ask him to create in you a desire for Christ that will surpass your desire for a spouse and every other earthly thing. This is a prayer he will surely answer. As your heart for Christ grows stronger, your contentment will deepen, because you will be receiving the desire of your heart. King David wrote, "Delight yourself also in the LORD, and He shall give you the desires of your heart" (Ps. 37:4).

THE LOVE OF YOUR LIFE

It is evident throughout Paul's letter to the Philippians that he was a man who suffered much worldly deprivation yet was nevertheless characterized by joy. He begins his letter, "I thank my God upon every remembrance of you, always in every prayer of mine making request for you all with joy" (Phil. 1:3–4).

Paul went on to tell the Philippians about his imprisonment for the sake of the gospel. He was bound in chains. That would be sufficient cause for depression and discouragement, yet Paul described it in this way: "But I want you to know, brethren, that the things which happened to me have actually turned out for the furtherance of the gospel, so that it has become evident to the whole palace guard, and to all the rest, that my chains are in Christ" (Phil. 1:12–13). Because Paul's heart was all for Christ, he saw his imprisonment as an advantageous circumstance!

He had joy over the spread of the gospel: "What then? Only that in every way, whether in pretense or in truth, Christ is preached; and in this I rejoice, yes, and will rejoice" (Phil. 1:18).

He had joy in self-sacrifice: "Yes, and if I am being poured out as a drink offering on the sacrifice and service of your faith, I am glad and rejoice with you all" (Phil. 2:17).

Paul wanted joy to characterize the lives of other believers: "Finally, my brethren, rejoice in the Lord" (Phil. 3:1a); and "Rejoice in the Lord always. Again I will say, rejoice!" (Phil. 4:4).

Paul found great joy in seeing the fruit of his labors on Christ's behalf: "Therefore, my beloved and longed-for brethren, my joy and my crown, so stand fast in the Lord, beloved" (Phil. 4:1).

He rejoiced in material provision when it came his way, regardless of delay: "But I rejoiced in the Lord greatly that now at last your care for me has flourished again, though you surely did care, but you lacked opportunity" (Phil. 4:10).

Such joy as Paul had is possible only for those whose hearts are set on Jesus Christ. If we look to our earthly lot for happiness, to other people to meet our needs, to whether we are being treated fairly and receiving the same blessings that others have, we will never know the contentment that Paul did. Those things won't ever come through for us, or, if they do, they will not provide us with the satisfaction that Paul knew. Only God and fellowship with him can satisfy the human heart and fulfill all desire. So if we seek it there, we will never be disappointed.

MAKING IT PERSONAL

Review

1. Why were bare necessities sufficient for Paul?

2. What means does God use to cultivate contentment in us?

For Personal Reflection or Group Discussion

1. Around what do you orient your life? The key to the real answer is found in your level of contentment. If you are discontent, then your life is oriented around something other than Christ.

2. What difficulties have you experienced as a result of being single? What have you learned about God in the process of working through those difficulties? Describe how these trials shaped you into the woman you are today.

3. Do you have a Christ-centered heart? Are you willing to have one if it means surrendering every aspect of your life to God? Sometimes we know a

particular thing is right and good, but in our heart of hearts we do not believe it. If you find yourself in that situation, sometimes the only place to begin is asking God to make you willing to be willing. Ask God to help you desire a Christ-centered heart above all else.

EPILOGUE

*W*e began by thinking about fine china and crystal—traditional bridal treasures. Yet through these seven chapters we have learned that biblical tradition can rule us rather than worldly custom. Therefore, one doesn't need to be a bride to acquire fine dishes for serving guests. Perhaps you already have a china pattern in mind along with plans for collecting place settings sufficient for a dinner party. Yet whether or not you decide to acquire china, you already possess the best treasure for serving guests, and that is Christ himself. Finer than gold-rimmed Limoges is a life committed to Christ and put to use for his glory. Offer your singleness to God. Ask him to use it in his redemptive plans in the place where he has set you. Allow him to take your singleness and make it beautiful. Let that be your finest china.

Deeper Insight from God's Word

Chapter 1: Longing for Love

Read through the Book of Job, and then answer the questions below based on the accompanying passages.

- What was Job's initial response when his life took a painful course? (Job 1:13–22; 2:7–10)

- How did Job's response change when his suffering was prolonged? (Job 3:1–26; 6:1–7:21; 13:20–27)

- What event immediately preceded the negative change in Job's outlook? (Job 2:11–3:1) How do you think this might have contributed to his depression?

- Job's three friends believed that Job was suffering because he had sinned in some way, but they were wrong. Not until the arrival of Elihu is this line of argument mitigated. How did Elihu steer Job down the right path? (Job 32–36)

- How was Job's outlook on his suffering changed after his thinking had been redirected up toward God? (Job 42:1–6)

- At what stage in the process of Job's suffering did God intervene to restore his fortunes? (Job 42:10)

- Did Job ever discover the purpose for his suffering?

Chapter 2: Safe in God's Sovereignty

1. According to 1 Peter 3:3–4 and 1 Timothy 2:9–10, what is true beauty? What basic principle is taught in these passages?

2. Read Joshua 15–19. As you read these chapters, notice that the land was not divided democratically. At God's decree, each tribe received a set portion, some larger, some smaller than the other tribes.

   - Why did the Levites receive no land? Read Deuteronomy 18:1–8 to find out.

   - Why was Simeon's portion established within the territory allotted to Judah? (Josh. 19:9).

   - What excuse did Ephraim and Manasseh give for not possessing their land? (Josh. 17:14–18) According to Joshua, what was necessary for these tribes to do in order to possess their land? What ungodly "foreign" influences are keeping you from possessing your land?

Chapter 3: A Right View of Reality

1. We tend to desire marriage as a means to personal happiness, but the New Testament teaches that its primary purpose is holiness, not happiness. Read the following passages about marriage: Matthew 19:3–12; 1 Corinthians 7:10–40; Ephesians 5:22–33; 1 Peter 3:1–6.

   - As women who can only respond to overtures of marriage rather than initiating them, how can we apply Jesus' words in Matthew 19:10–12?

   - In what ways did the apostle Paul have a realistic view of marriage? (1 Cor. 7:10–40)

   - What is the marital union meant to reflect? (Eph. 5:22–33)

   - What is the role of a wife designed to accomplish according to 1 Peter 3:1–6?

   - How does the New Testament picture of a biblical marriage alter your view of marriage as being the fulfillment of your desire for love, romance, and personal fulfillment?

   - As single women, how are we responsible to apply these passages in our lives?

2. Read the following passages about sexual intimacy: 1 Corinthians 6:12–20; 7:1–9.

   - According to Paul's teaching in 1 Corinthians 6:12–20, what happens at a spiritual level when a man and a woman are sexually intimate? What is the danger, therefore, in misusing it?

- In 1 Corinthians 7:1–9, Paul is advocating marriage as the legitimate outlet for sexual passion. If God has called you to singleness today (which he has, if you are single), then how can you glorify him with your innate sexual desires?

Chapter 4: The Blessings of a Thankful Heart

1. Read Psalms 18:16–19, 31:6–8, and 118:5–9. How does God respond when we entrust him with our distresses? Where does he take us when we submit to him? How is he our protector-deliverer in the midst of disappointment?

2. Read James 3:13–18 and 4:1–10.

   - James 3:13–18 offers a glimpse of the undercurrents in an envious heart. When envy is dominating our hearts, what is shaping our thoughts? What is the outcome of envy? How does this contrast with wisdom that comes from a God-centered heart and mind?

   - According to James 4:1–10, how do unrestrained desires lead to relational difficulties? What can hinder our ability to ask for and receive answers to prayer? What is the remedy James suggests?

Chapter 5: Day by Day

1. In John's Gospel we learn about a lonely woman who came to Jacob's well to draw water, a common household chore for the women in Jesus' day. This woman, a Samaritan, was living with a man to whom she was not married, and she'd had five husbands previously. Her personal history indicates a woman desperate for refuge, personal identity, and meaning in life. Read about her encounter with Jesus in John 4:1–30.

   • How did Jesus compare the two types of water? How did his illustration expose the true need of the Samaritan woman?

   • Why do you think Jesus brought her relationships with men into the conversation? In other words, how were those relationships relevant to their discussion?

Chapter 6: Understanding Your Unique Advantages

1. Mary Magdalene loved Jesus with great passion. He was the love of her life. Read Matthew 27:55–61; Mark 16:1–10; Luke 8:2–3; and John 20:1–20.

   • What circumstances fostered Mary's deep passion for Jesus?

2. Anna was a prophetess whose brief story appears in Luke 2:36–38.

• How was Anna set apart just for God? What special privilege did Anna receive as a result of living out her calling? The spiritual gift of prophecy was unique in ancient Israel, especially so among women. The role of prophetess was also a high calling. Anna recognized the privilege of being so gifted, and she dedicated her life to God's service in gratitude. Perhaps you've been given a unique calling as well, a calling that you and others recognize as a particular giftedness for the benefit of God's kingdom. If so, perhaps marriage would inhibit you from fully using that gift. In certain cases a call to missions is a good example. Marriage would have hindered Anna. Can you recognize your gift as a special privilege, a high calling? Are you humbled by the knowledge that God has singled you out for this purpose? Being single can indicate a call to do something uniquely special for God.

3. Read about Lydia and how she ministered to the apostles in Acts 16. Lydia was most likely a single woman, perhaps divorced or widowed, since no mention is made of a husband. She was a businesswoman, a seller of an expensive cloth dye called purple. Luke, the author of Acts, makes reference to Lydia by her profession, and from that we can infer that she was quite successful in her business.

- What gifts and talents do you find her exercising on behalf of the Christian community?

- How was Lydia in a position to use her financial acumen for the building up of the Christian community?

- What attitude and outlook on herself, her life, and God do you think enabled Lydia to be so fruitful?

Chapter 7: Establishing a Christ-Centered Life

The apostle Peter was a Christ-centered man, but he did not begin that way. At one point Peter even denied knowing Jesus because his desire to be liked and accepted by people was more important to him than standing by his faith. But Jesus restored Peter after his fall, and Peter learned in the process that nothing mattered to him as much as Christ. He gave his life over to promoting God's kingdom, a commitment that eventually cost him his life. Peter went from a scared disciple who denied his Lord, because he desired something else, to a man willing to die for Jesus. Learn about the spiritually mature Peter's outlook from the passages below.

- 1 Peter 1:3–9. How would you describe Peter's outlook? On what was he focused? What was his attitude about suffering?

- 1 Peter 2:9. How did Peter describe believers? Do you see yourself in the light of that reality?
- 1 Peter 2:11. Why do you think Peter referred to Christians as "sojourners and pilgrims"? What does this reveal about his view of this life?
- 1 Peter 4:1–2. What mindset did Peter advocate? How can the desire for marriage fall into the category of "the lusts of men"?
- 2 Peter 3:10–12. What outlook and focus motivated Peter to orient his life around Christ? What is the scope of your thoughts? What if Jesus were to return tomorrow morning (he might!)? As you contemplate that possibility, how does that affect your perspective on your marital status?

NOTES

Chapter 2: Safe in God's Sovereignty

[1] Dean R. Ulrich, "Lines in Pleasant Places: Joshua 15–19," *The Journal of Biblical Counseling* 18, no. 3 (spring 2000), 57.

[2] Elyse Fitzpatrick, *Idols of the Heart: Learning to Long for God Alone* (Phillipsburg, N.J.: P&R, 2001), 150.

Chapter 3: A Right View of Reality

[1] Michael J. McClymond, "Two Become One, Two Become Three: Pleasure and Procreation in Christian Understanding of Sex," *Modern Reformation*, November 2001, 16–21.

[2] Ibid., 20.

Chapter 5: Day by Day

[1] Joshua Harris, *I Kissed Dating Goodbye* (Portland, Ore.: Multnomah, 1997), 78.

Chapter 6: Understanding Your Unique Advantages

[1] Taken from a sermon preached by Philip Graham Ryken entitled "Second Honeymoon," based on the Book of Jeremiah, chapter 22.

[2] Susan T. Foh, *Women and the Word of God: A Response to Biblical Feminism* (Phillipsburg, N.J.: P&R, 1979) 128–29.

Lydia Brownback, a contented single woman, is the author of *Legacy of Faith*. She works for Alliance of Confessing Evangelicals in Philadelphia. There she produces The Bible Study Hour radio program and a daily devotional magazine. Having earned her M.A.R. degree at Westminster Theological Seminary in Philadelphia, she is involved in women's ministries at Tenth Presbyterian Church.